HOW TO HEAL THE INNER YOU

CONTENTS

For those who struggle through mental disorder,
mental health condition, and psychiatric disability.

You are not alone.

Let's do the work to shift your paradigm.

Let us heal.

MY EARLY ON SELF-DIAGNOSIS

So going back as far as adolescence for me, I don't know maybe it has been due to a change in hormones during that stage, but I tended to really suffer from anxiety, shyness, and even panic disorder. These conditions has all made themselves present in my life at those progressing times. I remember feeling awkward a lot and just flat out uncomfortable around other people. I was very shy, and tense and unaware of how I was supposed to act, which made me feel like I was a bit weird. I didn't understand at the time that we were all unique and that there was no right or wrong way to be. I was unaware of how to express myself. I was always worried about being judged, and I just felt like I did not matter at times. (mind you, this was me subconsciously doing this to myself) I would condition myself to stay quiet and not speak up because I wasn't even sure if I knew what I was talking about if I did so, this is why at school I would always choose a seat way in back of the classroom and hope not to be called on, I hoped to be phased out of the room and not noticed, but I was an observer, I will say that.

As I ambled on through my rising teenage years, my shyness and anxiety had joined me, when I was outdoors I just felt like everyone was all staring at me everywhere, from buses, to cars to the people walking pass and even the people across the street. So I was more of an introverted teenager, who would often hide away. Just did not want to be bothered with the company of others or the world period, cause then that would generate some sort of anxiety to me.

I had discomfort in being around other people and I had discomfort in just plain old living and experiencing the world. All of this was just too overstimulating psychologically. So we can all conclude that social anxiety ruled my world during these times. As I preceded into my adult years, just plain old anxiety period had took over my daily practice. I have accepted it as a part of my life, it has become a keen familiarity for me, and I could not proceed with my days in peace, there was always this inner voice refueling my anxiety, the inner voice has communicated to me consistently and it went something like this ''something crazy might happen today, and if it did not happen today then it might happen tomorrow , but you need to always be worried, don't be at peace, don't feel relaxed , be tense at all times, cause you just never know, it's coming I assure you''. This neurotic system was with me at all times [uninvited}.

So it made me feel like a weird person, like I was the only woman wandering around like this, like everyone else was normal and didn't have these thoughts, as my adult years pursued time. I gradually began to develop a curiosity about this condition I had. Why was I this way? Is there any way to change it? Can it get better? Will I ever experience a different way of being? Something has to give, I have to know.

I began searching/googling about the way I was feeling and to my surprise it wasn't only me but others was feeling the same way, yes, other people had anxiety too, just like I did. So my next curiosity would be, ok how to change it? Or is this just a way I am supposed to be? But,... is it? Let me google in ways to reverse anxiety disorder or to help combat it, where it cannot have control over me and my daily functions.

All of the answers that I've came across were to" identify a time, or a few times, in your past life that this type of conditioning may have sourced from," and there was nothing I had useful enough to come up with, other than me just being a shy kid. So as I had done more research, I came across another interesting observation, and here it is- many times we can inherit these problematic traits from our parents, and the environments we come from, while we are still in our mothers womb going through our formative development, we can pick up on the mothers painful emotional experiences and whatever her state of mind and being was at the moment of her pregnancy(during our time in the womb) any negative thoughts and feelings she has/had will be consumed by both her and the baby. Scientific research has confirmed that a women's nutritional condition, psychological states, and emotional inclination do in fact influence the susceptibility of the children she gives birth to. These traits often manifest as low self-worth, poor self-value, low self-esteem, and often a critical, negative review of themselves which then, persists on into adulthood.

Once I recognized this, I then contacted my mom, I wanted to ask her if these were some traits she may have been experiencing at the time of her pregnancy with me. I asked her what was some of her emotions while carrying me?, and she said that she was a teenager (17 years old) at the time of her pregnancy she felt nervous, scared, and uncertain, and a lot of anxiety. And there you have it, I consumed this as well, during my womb time. And as I gotten older it progressed, it developed into a disorder for me as well throughout my adult years.

So now I have this observation, my next mission is what can or what will I do to heal it? Inner healing is substantial, because these negative attributes are not supposed to be within us in the first place. They're altered states of being. So an important aspect I learned about inner healing is to take it one step at a time, what is some small goals I can set for each week, accomplish those, then set some more small goals different from the ones I had just accomplished. I researched on ways of how to heal my anxiety issues both social and general. Which brought me across these amazing systems for inner healing, I've compiled them together and I call them phases. They have worked wonders for me and my states of being. I want to share them with you. Let's get into it!

PHASE 1. DON'T RUSH THE PROCESS.

ealing yourself is a process that requires time, patience, and commitment. So we would start out by setting small objectives to promote progress. First, we want to acknowledge our emotions as they arise. Do not hide your feelings let them be, observe them, and that brings us to the next step of setting realistic expectations. Healing takes time, so be patient with the process and celebrate your small victories throughout this journey, for example; let's say, you appear to be a combative individual, the first step in this circumstance is understanding that you are hostile, now the second step would be to take a deep breath and keep your own emotions in checks. So to do this you would identify ways to implement a calm & collective mood for yourself, and stick to it consistently, ask yourself... what does it look like to have a slow reaction? this is where mindfulness comes in. All of these small practices that you've put into place should be acknowledged as gradual victories that will soon lead to milestones as long as you're consistent with them.

PHASE 2. TAKE CARE OF YOURSELF.

Self-care is an essential component of the healing process. Make sure to take care of yourself physically, emotionally, and mentally. This can include things like getting enough sleep, eating well, exercising, spending time in nature, practicing mindfulness, or engaging in activities that bring you joy. Practice self-compassion, remember that healing is a journey, and it's okay to stumble along the way. Treat yourself with the same kindness and compassion you would offer to a friend whom is going through a similar experience. Other examples of self-care might include pampering yourself, taking a bath, which can help to reduce stress levels. When you're less stressed, your body and mind are better able to cope with the healing process. Practicing self-care can also help to build resilience, which is the ability to bounce back from setbacks. You'll need this resilience to be able to take on the challenges that arise during the healing process. Another example of self-care would include engaging in creative pursuits, which can help to improve mood and reduce symptoms of depression and anxiety. You may also want to include activities such as journaling to help you to understand your thoughts, feelings, and behaviors. This can support personal growth and the healing process. Taking time out for yourself can help to boost self-esteem, which is the belief in your own worth and abilities. This can help to counteract negative self-talk and support a positive self-image. All of these self-care practices will help to increase energy levels which will support the healing process. As we can gather, self-care is vital for physical, emotional, and mental well-being, helping you to take care of yourself and make yourself a priority, which is essential for a successful healing journey.

PHASE 3. CONFRONT YOUR TRAUMA.

This can be a challenging and difficult process, but it can also be a powerful tool for healing, As this will help you to increase self-awareness. Once you confront this- it will likely help you become more aware of how it has affected your thoughts, feelings, and behaviors. This will help you understand yourself better and make more informed choices. You will become less likely to avoid the emotions and situations that are associated with it. This will help you feel more in control of your life and less overwhelmed. In the phase of confronting your trauma you will likely become prone to accept what has happened and the emotions that come along with it. This will help you move forward in the healing process. A direct result of experiencing a trauma is the struggling relationships that will now follow suit, and this is to no fault of your own-You have now inherited trust issues. In opposition, confronting this trauma can help you communicate more effectively with others and build more meaningful connections. You're likely to experience symptoms of anxiety, depression, and post- traumatic stress disorder (PTSD) as a result of the trauma directly, so when we build up that courage to confront the trauma it will lead to an improved quality of life, helping you feel more in control of your life and confident in your ability to handle challenges. If you feel the need to bring in the support of a mental health professional then that will be likely to implement a very important breakthrough for you.

PHASE 4. FORGIVENESS.

This will be a powerful tool for healing.

If you're reluctant to forgiveness this often implies that you're holding on to anger and resentment, and that can be detrimental to your physical and emotional health. Forgiveness can help to reduce these negative emotions, which can promote feelings of calm and well-being. You can count on the fact that this will improve relationships by helping to repair the damaged part of the relationship and also help to build stronger connections with others. When you forgive someone you're able to let go of past grievances and move forward in a more positive way. In the midst of building these stronger relationships, since we're practicing forgiveness it will give us the leverage to increase empathy, which is the ability to understand and share the feelings of others. This will lead to a more compassionate and understanding of relationships. Your stress levels will be reduced because you are no longer holding onto an exasperated emotion, which will promote clarity and mental freedom. Once we choose to forgive, we immediately start the healing process, now this would set out an awareness for us, helping to realize negative emotions and promote positive ones. This will also lead to improved physical and emotional health.

PHASE 5. MEDITATE.

Meditation has been shown to reduce stress levels by decreasing the production of stress hormones like cortisol and adrenaline. So incorporating meditation into a healing process can offer numerous benefits for physical and mental well-being, making it a valuable tool for promoting health and healing. Once you initiate the meditation practice you will soon learn how to regulate emotions and no longer feel stuck in a repetitive cycle of adverse feelings that aren't serving you well. This will help you manage your reactions to stressors. Meditate- be still- be present-, let thoughts flow, do not focus on them, when they come, let them come and then let them go, now you move back to the present moment, primarily focusing on your breathing and then your body- this practice of mindfulness ; which is the ability to stay present and aware in the moment is very instrumental for healing as it allows us to better recognize and understand our thoughts, feelings, and behaviors. This can be helpful in therapy as it allows individuals to often better recognize and understand their thoughts, feelings and behaviors. This will also help individuals who are in therapy to stay present and engaged during the session. Which can improve the effectiveness of the therapy. So we now know meditation is very beneficial in reducing stress levels, and the less stress we feel, the more effectively we can process and work through challenging emotions, this increased self-awareness can help us to identify patterns in our thoughts and behaviors. This amazing tool aids us in cultivating a sense of self compassion, and when we are more compassionate towards ourselves, we will be less critical and more accepting of our thoughts, feelings and behaviors, making it a valuable tool for promoting, emotional and psychological well-being.

PHASE 6. FIND YOUR SUPPORTIVE CIRCLE.

It is okay to ask for help. Consider seeking the support of a therapist, counselor, or other mental health professional. They can provide guidance, support, and tools to help you navigate the healing process. Or on a more personal note, you can gather a group of trusted individuals. Make sure these are people you trust and feel comfortable sharing your thoughts and feelings with(family members, friends, support groups). Through this supportive circle it's important to ensure these individuals will establish confidentiality, active listening, and mutual respect. You can also establish a supportive group through others you may meet or have met through therapy. If you're gaining a support circle from people you've met through therapy then it is essential you set intentions and guidelines to ensure everyone feel safe and supported. Share and listen, when its your turn to share- be honest and open about your feelings and experiences. Allow yourself to be vulnerable and trust that the group will hold space for you. When its someone else's turn to share, listen actively, and without judgement. another important aspect of healing through a supportive circle is the support that comes from others. Offer words of encouragement, validation, or simply hold space for someone as they process their emotions. One thing to keep in mind as we navigate through these phases is that healing is a process, and it's important to be patient with yourself and others as you continue to move forward, with a supportive circle you can feel empowered to take steps towards healing and growth.

PHASE 7. **LEARN TO LOVE.**

Learning to love yourself and others can be a powerful way to heal emotional wounds, and improve overall well-being. Instead of feeding a negative self-sabotaging thought system on a given day, make the choice to steer a different route and now, focus on the positive aspects of your life, even during difficult times. Take time each day to reflect on what you are grateful for. Surround yourself with people who uplift and support you, only give energy to the healthy relationships you have developed with others. When it comes to you, focus on the things you appreciate about yourself, make a list of the things you love about you and focus on that list, keep it with you everyday so you are reminded that you are loveable, and you matter. When we love ourselves we are more likely to take care of ourselves, set healthy boundaries, and make choices that align with our values and goals. It is important to prioritize self-love as a regular practice and to be patient with ourselves, as we learn to love ourselves more fully. This will also promote healthy relationships with others. This will be crucial in the healing process, as supportive relationships can provide a sense of comfort, validation, and encouragement.

PHASE 8. IDENTIFY YOUR BLESSINGS.

Take time to reflect; spend some time in quiet reflection, either alone or with someone you trust, to think about the ways in which you have been blessed during your healing journey. Consider both the big and small things that have brought you comfort, joy, or relief. Practice gratitude; make a conscious effort to focus on the positive aspects of your healing journey, rather than dwelling on the negative. Each day take time to write down three things you are grateful for related to your healing. Seek support; surround yourself with supportive people who can help you see the blessings in your healing process. Share your experiences with others who have gone through similar situations, join support groups, or seek professional counseling if needed. Focus on progress; celebrate each milestone in your healing journey, no matter how small. Recognize the progress you have made and the ways in which you have grown or learned from your experiences. Keep a positive mindset; maintain a positive attitude and focus on what you can do, rather than what you cannot. Remember that your mindset can have a powerful impact on your healing process. Keep in mind, healing is a journey and may not always be easy, but by focusing on the blessings in your life, you can find strength and inspiration to help you move forward.

PHASE 9. EMBRACE YOUR SPIRITUAL SIDE.

So we have found out from an earlier phase how important is to practice mindfulness, by now we should be making that a part of our daily practice, try to bring it into your schedule as often as possible. Connect with nature, this can be a great source of spiritual healing. Take a walk in the park, sit by a river, or spend some time in your garden. Reading spiritual texts can help you gain insight and inspiration. Consider reading texts from various spiritual traditions, such as the Bible, The Alchemist, The Power Of Now, etc. Engage in spiritual practices, make sure these practices align with your spiritual beliefs, such as prayer, yoga, or chanting. These practices can help you connect with your spiritual self and bring peace and comfort. Consider seeking guidance from a spiritual leader or counselor. Spiritual leaders can help you explore your spirituality and provide support as you navigate the healing process. Remember, the healing process is a journey, and there is no one right way to embrace your spiritual side, find what works best for you and trust in your own intuition.

PHASE 10. WHO DO YOU WANT TO BE?

Be open to new experiences; Healing often requires us to step outside of our comfort zones and try new things. Be open to new experiences and approaches to healing. Setting yourself up for new experiences can be very instrumental in helping you become truly who you desire to be, by engaging in new experiences different from your usual comfort zone, you will gain a different perspective towards life and what it can potentially offer you. The more you move away from your comfort zone and into different phases and directions, you will continuously boost confidence and a desire to seek more. Experiencing success in new and different situations can help you feel more confident in your abilities and strengths. So who exactly is it that you want to be? Identify the values that are important to you and align your actions with those values. This will help you stay true to yourself and your beliefs. Set goals; identify specific goals that align with the person you want to be and work towards achieving them. Break down larger goals into smaller, manageable steps, surround yourself with people who support and inspire you. this will help you stay motivated and encouraged on your journey. Embrace the change; be open to learning and growing, even when it is uncomfortable and challenging. Recognize that change is a natural part of the growth process. And remember; becoming the person you want to be is a journey, not a destination, celebrate your progress along the way, and be kind and patient with yourself as you navigate this process.

A FINAL WORD.

We know that healing is not always easy, but it is worth the effort. As long as you're committed to your healing journey and stay focused on your goals, even when things get tough, you are well on your journey to becoming who you want to be. Follow these phases and stay committed to them as this will imply that you're demonstrating faith. You believe in your healing even before it began. Real, lasting healing takes time and effort, and staying committed in this process means that you are prioritizing your healing journey and taking steps towards achieving long term healing and growth. You got this!!

Happy healing.

To all afflicted individuals who may feel physically, mentally or emotionally stagnant. There is a way out. Start from within.